GIFT WRAPPINGS

FOR EVERY OCCASION

Personalize your gifts with a wealth of inspirational ideas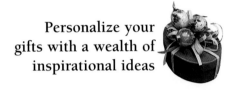

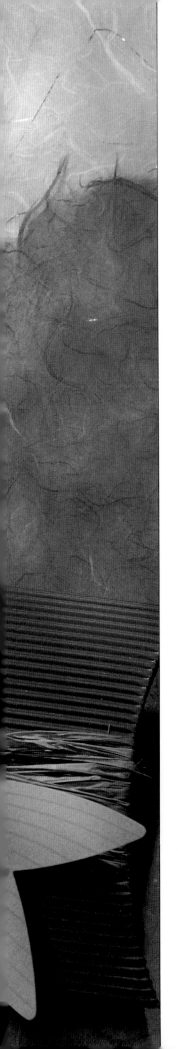

GILL DICKINSON

GIFT WRAPPINGS

FOR EVERY OCCASION

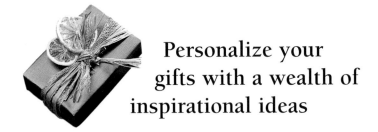

Personalize your
gifts with a wealth of
inspirational ideas

Grange
BOOKS

A QUANTUM BOOK

Published by Grange Books
An imprint of Grange Books plc
The Grange
Grange Yard
London SE1 3AG

ISBN 1-84013-048-2

QUMRAP

This book was produced by
Quantum Books Ltd
6 Blundell Street
London N7 9BH

Printed in Singapore by Star Standard Industries Pte. Ltd

CONTENTS

INTRODUCTION

There seem to be more and more occasions for exchanging gifts...
Christmas, birthdays, Easter, Hallowe'en, weddings, Valentine's Day,
Mother's Day... the list goes on. How many times have you complained
about the price of your shop-bought wrapping paper while hunting for
your scissors and sticky tape? How many times have you felt
disappointed when the wrapping on that expensive gift looks
uninspired and just plain untidy? Now you can learn how to make your
gift wrapping as beautiful and original as your gifts

*Home-made, decorated boxes and
envelopes make delightful, original gift
wrapping paper.*

*Crepe paper and paper fans are a
simple way of giving an oriental
flavour to your gift wrapping paper.*

Give a new lease of life to old carrier bags and boxes by gluing on plain or painted string patterns.

BE ORIGINAL

In the pages that follow you will find a wealth of inspirational ideas and techniques for creating dozens of different looks for your gifts. Whether you need to wrap a gift for a dedicated gardener – cover the wrapping paper with dried leaves and berries – or a fun gift for a child – make a giant pencil and fill it with novelty pens and pencils – there is an original idea to delight everyone.

NATURALLY BEAUTIFUL

The emphasis throughout is on using natural and recycled materials to create beautiful home made gift wrappings. There is no need to buy expensive ribbons, wrapping paper and gift tags when you can find an amazing range of materials and inspiration all around you: in your garden, on the beach or among the things you might otherwise throw away.

KEEP COLLECTING

Keep a box for your collection of gift wrapping accessories, from old buttons to odds and ends of ribbon and string. Whenever you take a walk along a beach or in a forest, keep an eye out for interesting natural objects such as shells, driftwood, seaweed, leaves, pinecones, berries and flowers. You will need to dry out leaves and flowers before using them – simply place them between layers of paper and weight them down for a couple of weeks.

FAMILY FUN

Most of the projects and techniques can be enjoyed by the whole family. Kids will love making their own wrapping paper and tags with potato printing, paint spattering and simple stencils. If you use recycled materials, by decorating plain brown paper for example, these techniques are also inexpensive. If you run out of ideas, you can always rely on your kids to think up something original!

PAPER, BOXES AND CONTAINERS

- Re-use paper whenever possible – tissue paper, brown paper and even old wrapping paper will come in useful. Spatter paint on to crumpled tissue paper for instant, original wrapping paper.
- Buy recycled or sugar paper from an art shop – these come in wonderful colours and are also very cheap.
- Keep an eye out for recycled metallic papers and cellophane – they have a softer, more natural look than non-recycled ones.
- Hold on to any boxes and containers you are given. Chocolates and biscuits often come in fancy packaging that can be repainted and decorated.
- Put awkward shaped presents in boxes before wrapping them – it makes it much easier to make the gift look good!
- Glass jars, even ordinary jam jars, are great for filling with home made sweets and truffles. Decorate with ribbons or paper cut-outs.
- Paint old pieces of corrugated card and wrap them around candles or bottles.
- Make simple sacks and bags from different materials, from muslin to hessian, for simple gift wrapping.
- Use envelopes and folders as another form of gift wrapping. Two templates are given – one for a simple, flat envelope and one for the 3D envelope used on page 27. Clear folders make fun gifts when filled with pretty stationery and pens.

A selection of decorated paper. The techniques used include stencilling and spattering.

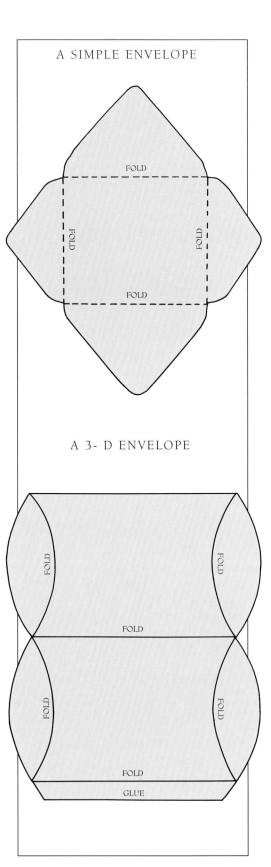

A SIMPLE ENVELOPE

FOLD

FOLD

FOLD

FOLD

A 3- D ENVELOPE

FOLD

FOLD

FOLD

FOLD

FOLD

FOLD

GLUE

STRING, RIBBON AND WIRE

• Before buying expensive ribbons, have a look in your garden shed or tool box – garden twine, raffia, string and wire are all cheap and have great textures.

• Paper ribbon comes in wonderful colours and, when unravelled, makes very impressive bows.

• As an alternative to silky ribbons, try paper and cotton braid.

• Paint on some extra decorations or pierce a pattern in paper braid.

• You will need some different thicknesses of florist's wire when working with dried flowers and berries.

PAINT, SCISSORS AND GLUE

• Try to form a collection of different paints in a range of colours. For most jobs poster paints will work well. Gouaches are useful for finer details – when decorating eggs or for fine stencils. Oil paints are useful for the marbling paper technique.

• You will also need a range of paint brushes including stencilling brushes. Keep an old tooth brush for paint spattering. Household paint brushes are good for covering large areas quickly.

• Use masking fluid – (don't give it to young children) – to create interesting "resist" effects on paper, card and even eggs!

• Use scissors where possible. If necessary, use a scalpel, but take care and always use a cutting mat. Pinking shears are useful for instant and interesting paper effects.

• You will need some white, all-purpose craft glue capable of sticking paper, card, fabric, plastic and string. This takes an hour or so to dry, so some quick-drying clear adhesive will also be useful.

• Avoid spray adhesives. These are not very effective for anything other than paper and are not very safe or environmentally friendly.

• You will also need masking tape, double-sided sticky tape and ordinary sticky tape.

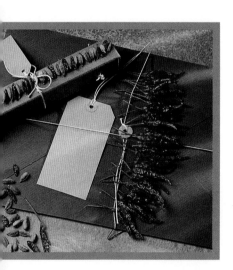

These gifts have a fresh, natural look. The packages were tied with string and the chillies were threaded on to florist's wire.

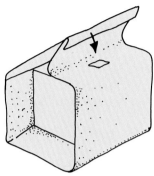
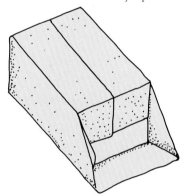
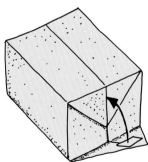

Chapter One

BACK TO NATURE

Seeds, pods, spices and fruit dry easily and quickly. They make fragrant and beautiful additions to your gifts as well as great Christmas tree decorations. Prepare fruit and spices in Autumn so you have a wealth of material ready for the festive season. A single layer of citrus slices and spices kept in a warm, dry place will be ready to use in three to four weeks. Fresh and dried herbs and spices can be brought from supermarkets and specialist food stores. Co-ordinate this natural look by using green and brown boxes, raffia and string.

1 Thread slices of citrus fruits, bay leaves and bunches of cinnamon sticks on to a length of raffia. Tie on some heart-shaped cookies. Attach this gorgeous garland to your wrapped box.

2 Tie natural raffia around a box and decorate with a heart-shaped cookie.

3 Tie a box with ribbon and green raffia and decorate with sliced oranges and lemons.

STRING, RIBBON AND WIRE

• Before buying expensive ribbons, have a look in your garden shed or tool box – garden twine, raffia, string and wire are all cheap and have great textures.

• Paper ribbon comes in wonderful colours and, when unravelled, makes very impressive bows.

• As an alternative to silky ribbons, try paper and cotton braid.

• Paint on some extra decorations or pierce a pattern in paper braid.

• You will need some different thicknesses of florist's wire when working with dried flowers and berries.

PAINT, SCISSORS AND GLUE

• Try to form a collection of different paints in a range of colours. For most jobs poster paints will work well. Gouaches are useful for finer details – when decorating eggs or for fine stencils. Oil paints are useful for the marbling paper technique.

• You will also need a range of paint brushes including stencilling brushes. Keep an old tooth brush for paint spattering. Household paint brushes are good for covering large areas quickly.

• Use masking fluid – (don't give it to young children) – to create interesting "resist" effects on paper, card and even eggs!

• Use scissors where possible. If necessary, use a scalpel, but take care and always use a cutting mat. Pinking shears are useful for instant and interesting paper effects.

• You will need some white, all-purpose craft glue capable of sticking paper, card, fabric, plastic and string. This takes an hour or so to dry, so some quick-drying clear adhesive will also be useful.

• Avoid spray adhesives. These are not very effective for anything other than paper and are not very safe or environmentally friendly.

• You will also need masking tape, double-sided sticky tape and ordinary sticky tape.

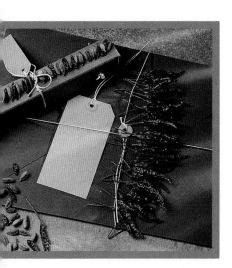

These gifts have a fresh, natural look. The packages were tied with string and the chillies were threaded on to florist's wire.

WRAPPING A BOX

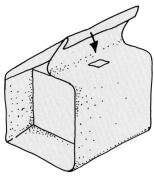

1 Cut the paper to fit the box. You will need an overlap at the top of about 10cm (4in) and two thirds the box height at the sides. Fold down the top by 2cm (3/4in) from the edge. Centre the fold on the box and hold down with double-sided sticky tape.

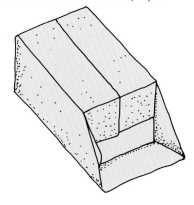

2 Centre the box in the paper and press the folded edge against the box. Crease the side folds before pushing them in.

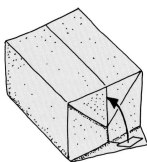

3 Fold up the triangular fold and fix with double-sided sticky tape. Repeat at the other end of the box.

Chapter One

BACK TO NATURE

Seeds, pods, spices and fruit dry easily and quickly. They make fragrant and beautiful additions to your gifts as well as great Christmas tree decorations. Prepare fruit and spices in Autumn so you have a wealth of material ready for the festive season. A single layer of citrus slices and spices kept in a warm, dry place will be ready to use in three to four weeks. Fresh and dried herbs and spices can be brought from supermarkets and specialist food stores. Co-ordinate this natural look by using green and brown boxes, raffia and string.

1 Thread slices of citrus fruits, bay leaves and bunches of cinnamon sticks on to a length of raffia. Tie on some heart-shaped cookies. Attach this gorgeous garland to your wrapped box.

2 Tie natural raffia around a box and decorate with a heart-shaped cookie.

3 Tie a box with ribbon and green raffia and decorate with sliced oranges and lemons.

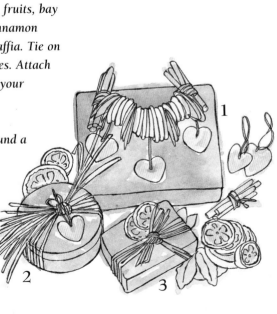

FRUIT AND SPICE

A selection of dried fruit, seed and spice decorations. The method for making the spice balls is shown on page 19. Make some hearts from florist's wire and thread on dried cranberries and cardamoms.

Tie some dried oranges, raffia and berries into a bunch and attach to a natural straw heart. You can hang this from a mantelpiece or door or simply tie on to a gift.

HOT AND SPICY

You can buy chillies ready dried or dry them yourself. Red chillies look great on gold boxes and bags. Thread together some small chillies for a small gift. Use a couple of large chillies on a bigger present.

Decorate a large envelope with a garland of dried chillies and a brown label. Thread tiny chillies and cardamoms alternately on to string and tie on to a box.

SPICE BALLS

These beautiful, fragrant spice balls make a colourful
and exotic addition to any gift. Fill a plain brown box
with a selection of cooking spices or pot pourri, tie
with natural-coloured raffia and attach a spice ball.

*1 Push a length of wire into a
polystyrene ball and fold in one
end of the wire to make a small
loop. Draw a spiral of glue around
the ball. Carefully stick on the
sunflower seeds.*

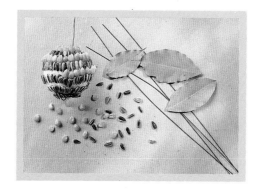

*2 When this glue has dried, draw
a second spiral of glue on to the
ball. Decorate with dried corn
kernels. Leave the ball to dry
completely.*

*3 Thread some raffia through the
loop on the base of the ball.
Repeat at the top, leaving enough
raffia for hanging the ball. Glue
on some dried bay leaves*

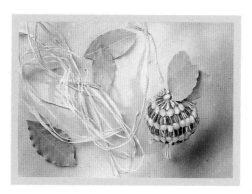

GINGERBREAD

Make some gift bags extra special by using some home made gingerbread. Use dried cranberries, bay leaves and chillies for extra decoration. This is a fun project for the family to tackle together.

INGREDIENTS
75g/3oz soft brown sugar
30ml/1 tbsp golden syrup
15ml/1 tbsp molasses
30ml/1 tbsp water
100g/4oz butter
½tsp baking soda
200g/8oz plain flour
5ml/1 tsp ground ginger
5ml/1 tsp cinnamon

1 Bring the sugar, syrup, molasses and water to the boil, stirring well.

2 Remove the pan from the heat and add the butter and baking soda. Stir in the flour and spices and mix well.

3 Leave the dough for 1 hour. Preheat the oven to 180°C/350°F/Gas Mark

4 Bake the gingerbread for 10–12 minutes. Pierce holes for hanging while the cookies are still warm. Cool on a wire tray.

1 Decorate a red bag with a paper ribbon bow, raffia and decorated gingerbread.

2 Decorate a blue bag with threaded chillies and cinnamon sticks.

3 Decorate gingerbread with cranberries and bay leaves and tie on to a bag.

4 Thread cranberries on to a wire heart and tie on to some gingerbread with raffia.

Chapter Two

BESIDE THE SEASIDE

A walk along the seashore will produce a wealth of both inspiration and materials for your gift wrapping. The textures and colours of natural objects such as shells, pebbles and stones, seaweed and driftwood make beautiful additions to presents and help you to create unique gifts with very little effort. Alternatively, decorate your gifts with shapes from the undersea world – fish and seahorses for example – the choice is limited only by your imagination.

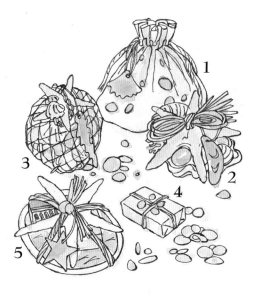

1 Make a simple drawstring bag in natural fabric and cover with stones. Finish with a shell label.

2 Fill a large shell with gifts for the bathroom, tie with raffia and add a tag.

3 Fill a string bag with shells and natural sponges. Decorate with a star fish.

4 Wrap a small bar of soap in natural-coloured paper and tie with raffia. Decorate with stones.

5 A round loofah makes a good base for a present; finish off with raffia and a star fish.

PAPERS

These delicate tissue papers have been decorated with relief fabric paint. The paints are very easy to draw with and can be used directly from the tube. Create a simple seashore pattern, seaweed and shells for example, and add some small pieces of torn tissue for extra decoration.

TAGS

The gold and white tags and wooden fish were sold as decorations for Christmas trees but they make stunning additions to gifts. Simple fish and shell shapes can be cut out from paper and decorated with spattered paint or strips of tissue paper. A few templates are given on page 114-115. You can also make small cuts in the tags to give a little more texture.

DECORATING WITH SHELLS

1 Stitch together two pieces of white muslin to make a bag. Using clear glue, stick on small shells, fill the bag with bath salts and tie the top with raffia.

2 Wrap boxes and soaps with white muslin and again decorate with shells and raffia. Place small presents on a large flat shell to make more of an impact.

BENEATH THE WAVES

These simple boxes were made from corrugated cardboard. You can find the pattern for this type of box on page 13. Decorate the boxes with paper fish (template on page 114-115). Decorated boxes are an ideal way of presenting difficult shapes such as ties and scarves

TORN PAPER

Overlapping layers of torn paper give an
interesting textured look to a gift. You can use
either bought papers or decorate your own.
Tissue paper is ideal since it comes in a
wonderful range of colours, it is translucent and
is cheap.

*1 Cover a box with tissue and decorate
with torn paper, raffia and shells.*
*2 Wrap a box with turquoise and torn
paper. Decorate with torn paper.
Decorate with pieces of raffia and a
chocolate fish.*
*3 Use speckled paper to wrap a box,
decorate with torn paper, raffia and a
star fish.*
*4 Decorate a box with silver mesh
fabric, raffia and novelty chocolate fish.*

*1 Wrap the box with blue
tissue paper. Tear off two strips
of light blue textured paper
and wrap around the gift,
securing with sticky tape.*

*2 Choose two colours of tissue
paper. Tear off a mixture of
small and large strips and glue
to the box.*

*3 Wrap coloured raffia around
the middle of the box, tying it
at the back with a knot.
Decorate with shells.*

Collect shells whenever you go on holiday. When you travel to exotic locations, make sure you do not take away rare shells that may be protected by law. Complement these naturally beautiful objects by using hand made and recycled papers to wrap your gifts. A beautiful hand made box is a wonderful gift in itself and can be filled with bath salts, soaps or simply more shells.

1 *Wrap a strip of paper ribbon around a textured paper carrier bag and decorate with grass and shells.*
2 *Use a small amount of clear adhesive to attach shells directly to a small bag.*

3 *Thread shells or sea urchins on to a piece of raffia. Attach to the lid of a box.*
4 *Personalize some bought paper and envelopes by decorating with shells. Pierce a hole in the shell with a needle and thread with raffia.*

Chapter Three

PERFECT PAPER

Paper is a very versatile medium. You can create wonderful three-dimensional and textured effects with simple techniques. Both children and adults will enjoy folding, cutting, creasing, curling and pleating papers to create original and inexpensive gift wrapping. You will need some fine to medium-weight papers in a range of colours, scissors or a scalpel, a cutting mat and glue or sticky tape.

1 Lightly fold plain paper around the box. Lay it flat again and mark out the circular pattern in pencil on two box sides only. Cut out the pattern with a scalpel. Wrap the box and decorate with shredded paper.

2 A small present can look effective by cutting a pattern in only part of the paper. Add a cut-paper tag.

3 A coloured box showing through cut paper gives an interesting effect.

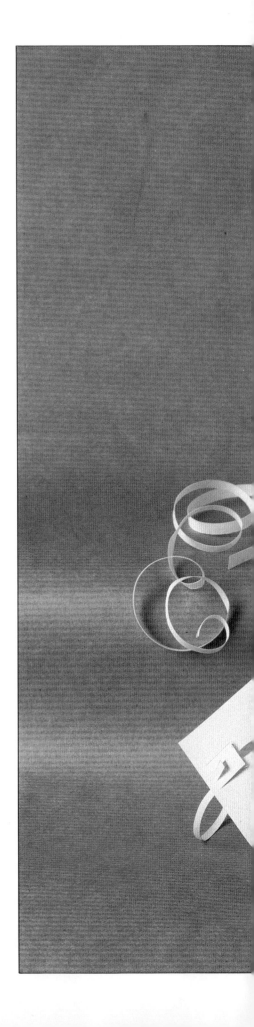

CUT PAPER I

A simple cut-out pattern like these regularly spaced
squares gives an interesting effect with little effort.
You will need a cutting mat, scalpel, ruler and pencil.
Draw a simple grid making sure that when you cut
the squares they do not run into each other.

CUT PAPER II

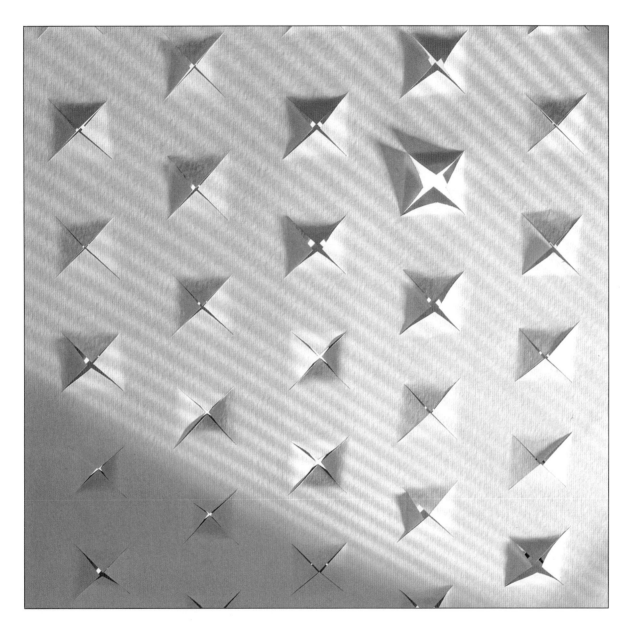

You can make a cut-paper pattern as complicated as you wish. Mark out another square grid but this time cut the diagonals, not three sides of the square. Use a steel rule and a sharp blade if possible.

FLOWER POWER

Make a card by folding some hand made or embossed
paper in half. Cut out a vase from plain white paper and
cut two rows of small "v" shapes across the top. Glue the
sides of the vase to the card. Cut out some flower and
leaf shapes and glue or tape these inside the vase.

WHITE WEDDING

Use medium-weight paper for this larger cutwork
wrapping paper. Repeat the triangular pattern on the
tag. The decorative bow is made by holding strips of
paper and attaching them to the top of the box. Use a
sharp blade to achieve clean, sharp lines.

PRETTY IN PINK

Wrap presents in pretty pastel papers and add strips
of co-ordinating colours. Add extra interest by cutting
the edges of the paper into zig zags and curves or use
pinking shears. Make some matching flowers as
shown on page 40.

PLEASING PASTELS

Cut several leaves and flowers (see page 116-117) from lightweight paper. Pierce a hole in the centre of the flowers and thread on to 2.5cm/1in of rolled up paper. Glue on to the gift with some paper leaves.

Make some simple co-ordinating tags for these gifts. You will need some matching papers, all of similar weight, scissors, pinking shears, a hole punch and glue. Make some small flowers for extra decoration.

PAPER FLOWERS

A simple gift of stationery can be made extra special by wrapping decorative strips of coloured paper around the centre. Add a pencil or biro decorated to look like a flower and a leaf tag.

1 Cut several strips of coloured paper and cut patterns along the edges. Wrap these around the gift. Wrap a pencil or pen in green paper.

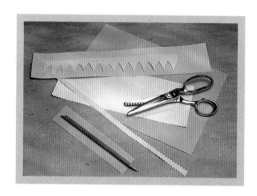

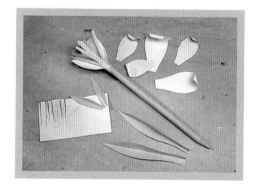

2 Cut out several petal shapes in paper and curl over the ends. Cut a 5cm/2in strip of paper and make cuts in it (templates on page 116-117). Wrap around the pencil and then glue on the petals one by one.

3 Cut out some leaf shapes and glue on the pencil. Cut a leaf for the tag, make a hole and thread through a thin strip of paper for attaching to the gift.

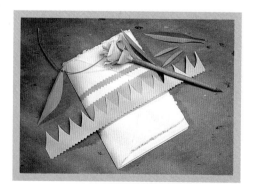

A home made cracker makes a very special gift. The method is shown on page 70. Choose the materials and colours to reflect the occasion – in this case pastel and white papers. The traditional wedding almonds are tied in white net and placed on decorated crepe paper.

Keep a collection of boxes and containers for your gift wrapping. Cover a box in lightweight paper and decorate with cut-out shapes and paper flowers.

Chapter Four

GIFTS FROM THE HEART

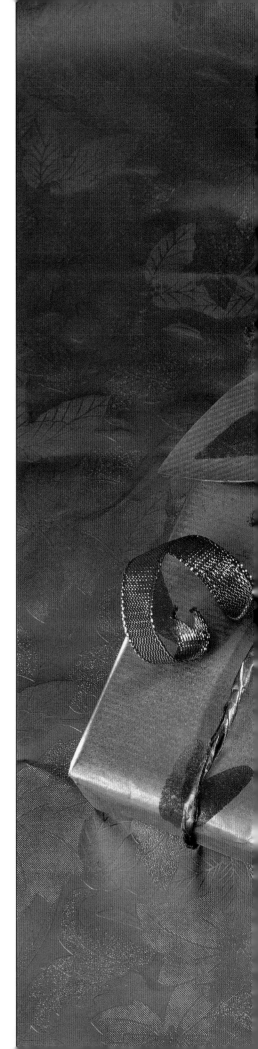

The heart is a symbol of love and friendship. Heart images can be used on gifts for many different occasions – for Mother's Day, a wedding, a Christening and, of course, for Valentine's Day. Hearts can be very decorative or simple, symmetrical or more stylized. The inspirational ideas that follow range from a simple heart-shaped box with a hand made tag to wire hearts threaded with flowers. Look out for old heart-shaped boxes and containers that can be repainted or decorated.

1 Stencil red hearts on to gold paper and use matching gold paper ribbon and tag.

2 Stencil gold hearts on to a red heart-shaped box and add a bow made of fine strands of ribbon and a beaded tag.

3 Tie a round box with two different thicknesses of ribbon. Add a wooden tag that has been decorated with fabric relief paint.

PAPERS

These three papers were made using a very simple piercing technique, described on page 52. Designs can be repetitive or random and the sizes of the holes can be varied to emphasize different areas of the design. Any simple shape or pattern works well.

SWEET HEARTS

Instead of buying a box of chocolates, make or buy some heart-shaped truffles, place on a heart-shaped plate and wrap with cellophane. Decorate with transparent ribbon and a heart tag. Make a card from recycled paper, glue gauze ribbon down the front and tie on a paper heart with raffia. The wooden heart has been decorated with dried flowers and raffia and can be tied on to a present.

Dried flowers are a very simple way of decorating a gift. It can also be very economical if you have a well stocked garden. Most florists have a large selection of dried flowers and they can advise on which fresh flowers dry well – roses, hydrangeas, lavender, bay leaves and sunflowers are just a few examples. Look out for unusual boxes and baskets made in natural materials such as cane and willow. Flowers not only make wonderful, long-lasting gifts, but they also smell delicious.

1 *Fill a hollow wooden heart with lavender and decorate with dried sunflower heads.*

2 *Place some painted heart boxes on top of each other and secure with paper ribbon. Decorate with sprigs of lavender, roses and bay leaves.*

3 *Tie small bunches of lavender together with wire and cut the stems 4cm–1½ in from the flowers. Tie the bunches around the edge of a heart-shaped basket with pieces of wire, filling in all the gaps.*

HEARTS AND FLOWERS

These delicate miniature wreaths make beautiful presents in themselves but can also be added to other gifts. Make a simple heart shape from florist's wire and decorate with any flowers you have to hand. Pierce rosebuds with a needle and thread on to the wire. Glue rose petals on to a wire heart and decorate the top with flowers. For a large heart, make small bunches of grasses, flowers and leaves and tie on to the heart with more wire.

PURPLE HEARTS

Carefully co-ordinate all the elements of your gifts – wrapping paper, ribbon, tag and card. Make each gift more special by adding your own decoration to the shop-bought elements.

1 *Wrap individual soaps with recycled papers and tie with cotton ribbons decorated with fabric relief paint. Place the gifts in a wire soap dish and add a home made lavender bag.*

2 *Make your own card with hand made paper. Cut one heart from corrugated card and tear another from purple recycled paper. Thread a gold wire heart through the corrugated card.*

PIERCED PAPER

The technique of piercing paper can be used for wrapping papers, tags, ribbons and cards. The delicate effect is achieved by piercing the paper with the fine point of a needle or nail. Although hearts have been used here, any simple design will be effective.

1 *Take two pieces of coloured paper and two sizes of heart stencil (see page 114-115). Cut out one of each size.*

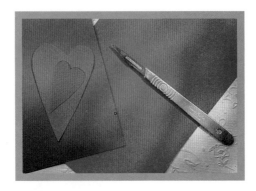

2 *You will need two sizes of needle. Lay your hearts on a soft blanket and pierce the edge of the larger heart with the thicker point.*

3 *Repeat the process with the smaller heart and needle. Pierce a hole through the top of both hearts and thread with a ribbon.*

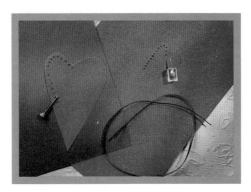

Wrap boxes in corrugated card and decorate with pierced paper ribbon and tags. Glue some small hearts on to pieces of wire and gather into a bunch to decorate the gifts.

STRAIGHT TO THE HEART

Dress up some simple boxes (above) with a few little personal touches. Decorate ribbon with fabric relief paint and make your own tag; cut out one large heart outline and tie on a smaller pierced paper heart with raffia.

Make some original paper by stencilling large white hearts on to some bought red paper. Make a matching red and white tag. Wrap a box (left) with the paper and tie with white paper ribbon. Decorate with a chocolate heart.

TAGS

The metal tags were originally meant to hang on Christmas trees, but will enhance any Valentine's Day gift. The pierced paper tags range from simple designs to complicated patterns. The wooden tags have been decorated by gluing on a few heart sequins, stencilling on heart shapes or adding a small bunch of dried flowers.

Chapter Five

AUTUMN LEAVES

Leaves are a wonderful form of natural decoration. They come in all shapes, sizes and colours and, best of all, are completely free! Collect leaves all year round – on country walks, in the back garden or along your route to work or school – place them between layers of newspaper and weight down with books for about two weeks. You will be left with a large selection of shapes to use for labels, paper and decoration. When using leaf motifs, reflect the shades of autumn, from soft greens, ochre and burnt sienna to browns and gold. Use natural colours of raffia or string.

1 Wrap boxes in paper spattered with autumnal coloured paints and tie with string. Make more of a small gift by placing it on a large cut-out leaf.

2 Wrap gifts with brown paper and tie with raffia or string. Spatter the whole present with gold paint and decorate with a metal leaf tag.

PAPERS

These spattered and stencilled papers have been made on a range of paper thicknesses and types. Medium-weight hand made papers can be used and look wonderful with natural forms stencilled on to them. Spattered papers are made by placing leaves randomly on paper and securing them with double sided tape. Spatter (see page 64) with a mixture of rich greens and lift off the leaves when dry. Use the leaves for labels or extra decoration.

TAGS

A mixture of decorative leaf shapes. Real leaves can be used as templates for cutting shapes out of brown paper. Paint or spatter the paper leaves with gouache or poster paint, or leave brown. Punch a hole in the tag and thread through string or raffia to tie to the present.

STENCILLING

The key to stencilling is using a dry brush. This will give good results and helps the stencil to last. Tie your wrapped boxes with raffia. Any scraps of stencilled paper can be added to a plain present to give a different look.

1 Choose an interesting leaf and draw around it on to medium-weight paper, leaving a good sized border for neat stencilling.

2 Cut out the leaf carefully. If you do not want to use a scalpel, copy one of the templates from pages 118–119 on to a piece of paper, fold in half and cut out with scissors.

3 Mix the paint to a thick consistency and keep the brush dry. Lay the stencil over the paper and lightly dab the paint evenly. Use two colours for a richer effect.

 You can collect natural items, such as leaves, pine cones and berries, all year round. You should also keep an eye out for unusual gifts, particularly when travelling abroad. A bundle of these twig pencils with a spattered leaf tag makes a great, natural-style gift. Alternatively, just one pencil placed under the bow of a present with the tag attached adds an extra special touch.

1 The recycled paper used here is cheap and makes great gift wrap. Stick real leaves on to the paper and glue several into a bunch to decorate the top of the present.

2 Cut oak leaf shapes out of brown paper and paint with a mixture of oranges and greens. When glued onto the wrapped box they give an interesting three-dimensional effect. Add a green raffia bow.

SPATTERING

Spattering is a simple decorative technique. You need a selection of gouache or poster paints, paper and an old toothbrush or stencilling brush. For these gifts brown paper has been spattered with paint, tied with raffia and string, and decorated with real and cut-out spattered leaves. Dried twigs and berries have been added for final decoration.

1 Take a real leaf, draw around it and cut out of paper. Alternatively, use one of the leaf templates on pages 118–119. Select some autumnal colours and mix them to a medium consistency.

2 Dip the toothbrush in the first colour and run your finger across the bristles to produce a fine spray effect. Repeat with other colours. Punch a hole and add a raffia or string tie.

Chapter Six

A COUNTRY CHRISTMAS

 Giving and receiving presents is an important part of the Christmas celebrations. Tartan and checked patterns will give a traditional, rustic look to your gifts especially when you enhance them with heather, pine-cones and nuts. You can use a range of different patterned materials from wrapping paper and paper napkins to hessian and tartan cloth. Children love finding a stocking of presents on Christmas morning. They are simple to make – the template is on page 122-123 – and you can use any material you have to hand. Decorate them with buttons, beads and ribbon.

1 Make the basic stocking in yellow fabric with a contrasting blue checked top and Christmas trees.

2 Use blue checked fabric as the base and add a green top and details in red checked fabric.

3 Make a blue and tartan stocking. Add a tartan pocket and bows made from checked cloth and raffia.

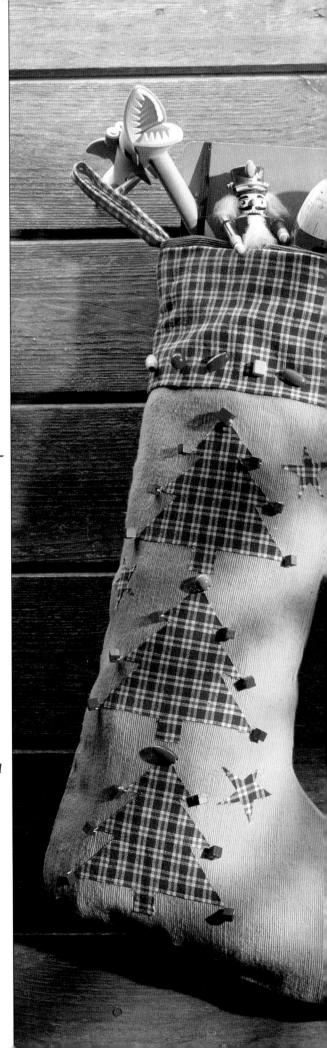

You can solve the problem of wrapping bulky and awkwardly shaped gifts by putting them in simple fabric bags.

Bags disguise the shape of a present such as a bottle and look fun and interesting. A combination of tartan, checked and hessian fabrics will give a fresh, natural look to your gifts. Using up scraps of fabric is also an economical form of gift wrapping. Complement the country look by fraying the edge of the fabric, tying the gifts with natural string and adding home made tags.

1 Fold a piece of hessian in half and sew up the sides to make a bag. Sew a strip of fabric to the top of the bag. Stitch along the top and bottom edges and thread string through the gap between the two edges.

2 To wrap a bottle, make a narrow bag and tie the top with fabric. Make a matching tag by gluing fabric on to a card tag (template pages 126-127).

3 Decorate a hessian bag with some checked-fabric Scottie dogs (a template is on page 123).

4 Decorate jars filled with home made goodies with strips of hessian and contrasting fabrics.

CHRISTMAS CRACKERS

Crackers are part of a traditional Christmas and a home made one also makes an unusual form of gift wrapping. You can put any small gift in the middle from novelty hats and toys to something really special.

1 Cut a piece of paper 34 x 18cm/13½ x 7in. Cut a piece of thin card 9 x 18cm/3½ x 7in. Cut two pieces of thin card 7 x 18cm/ 2 ¾ x 7in. Stick some lace along the short edges of the paper.

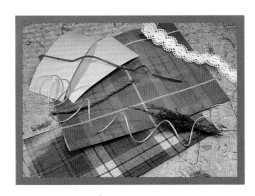

2 Roll the larger piece of card into a tube and place in the middle of the paper. Put your gifts and the "snap" in the tube and fasten the paper around. Tie each end with string. Open out the ends of the paper and insert the smaller tubes.

3 Thread some paper lace on to two pieces of wire and gather it up. Tie around the "joints" of the cracker and secure with tape. Decorate the middle and ends with ribbon and heather.

Wrap your boxes with tartan-patterned paper to give an instant festive look and add rich, co-ordinating paper-ribbon bows.

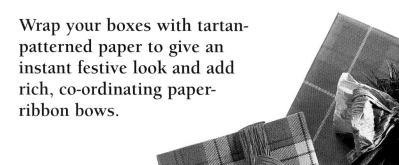

Tie your tartan presents with paper ribbon, heather and thistles. Decorate the lid of a wooden box with moss, nuts, cinnamon and pine-cones.

Paper napkins make cheap and fun gift wrapping. Make some simple bags by gluing the sides of a napkin together and tie the top with string and sweets. These make great going-home presents for a children's party.

1 Wrap a piece of corrugated card around several thin candles or one large candle. Add cut-out holly leaves (template page 120) and tartan-ribbon bows.

2 Tie some candles together with a tartan bow and a holly leaf made from card. Make a drawstring bag from tartan fabric, fold over the top and stitch down. Thread through a piece of string.

A gift wrapped in fabric makes a great change from paper-wrapped gifts. Tartan fabrics are rich in both colour and texture. Complement the natural look by adding bows made from cotton braids in dark, rich colours. Fresh berries, nuts and pine-cones make wonderful additional decorations. Keep your eye out for remnants of fabric, which are often sold very cheaply. Keep all your scraps of fabric since these can be used as ribbons or for making small bags for lavender and soap. Shop-bought corn decorations go well with these tartan gifts.

1 Cover a box with tartan fabric and tie with cotton braid. Decorate with berries, pine-cones and pine leaves.

2 Fold a rectangle of tartan fabric in half and stitch the sides together. Tie the top with string and add some corn decorations.

3 Wrap a box with fabric and decorate with nuts and pine-cones. Wrap florist's wire around the base of the pine-cones and push the wire into the eye of each nut. Secure with glue.

Chapter Seven

ENCHANTING EASTER GIFTS

Easter, in the western hemisphere, coincides with the beginning of spring and the end of the cold, grey winter months. This is the time of year when the flowers burst into life and the mass of colours these produce make them wonderful Easter gifts. Keep an eye out for unusual pots and baskets for your flowers, plants and bulbs - why not use a large china cup and saucer. Use your imagination to make more of traditional Easter eggs. Use delicate quail's eggs, paint them if you wish, as extra decoration or fill a pretty basket with miniature foil-covered chocolate eggs. Create some original gifts by painting hen's eggs with your own designs.

1 Fill a shaped basket with potted daffodils and cover with fresh moss.

2 Fill a wooden trough or a china cup, saucer and plate with primroses.

3 Fill small terracotta pots with snowdrops and chocolate eggs. Decorate with sugared primroses.

4 Wrap a bunch of flowers in yellow tissue paper and tie with a ribbon.

PAPERS AND TAGS

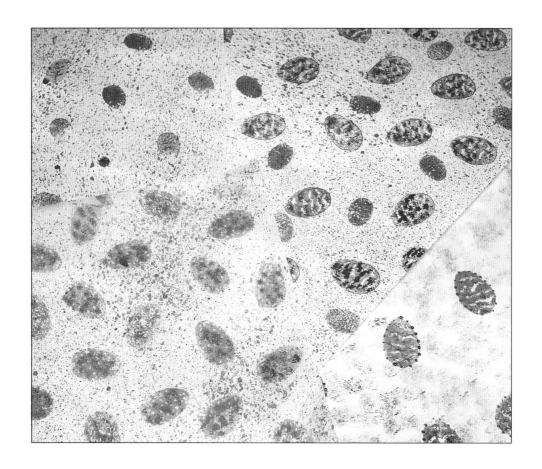

A selection of papers decorated with paint spattering and potato-print patterns (see page 80).

A mixture of bought metal tags and hand made paper ones. You will find Easter templates on pages 124-125. Decorate with paint spattering and cut-outs.

GLORIOUS GLASS

Fill glass preserving jars and pots with chocolate eggs,
sweets and nuts. Decorate with paper cut-out
patterns, raffia bows and paper tags. You will find a
few Easter templates on pages 124-125.

POTATO PRINTING

Potato printing is a simple way of decorating paper and cards. The whole family can enjoy creating a range of different effects. Buy textured papers or create an interesting base paper by first spattering paint finely over the paper. Any thickness of paper is suitable, but tissue papers look particularly good. Choose a simple design and cut it out cleanly for best results.

1 Cut a medium-sized potato in half. Cut a stencil for your design from card and then trace it on to the potato surface. Cut around the shape carefully with a knife or scalpel.

2 Mix poster paints or gouaches to a medium consistency and brush sparingly on to the potato. Press the potato evenly down on to the paper.

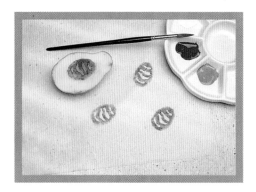

Cover boxes with spattered and potato-printed paper. Tie with silky ribbons, add some quail's eggs and a hand made tag. Fill some pretty baskets with coloured, natural and chocolate eggs.

Weaving paper is another simple technique that is great for gift wrapping: for tags, cards or carrier bags. Use any type of paper you have to hand - newspaper, crepe, tissue or hand made papers. You can achieve a range of effects by weaving only parts of the paper or by using a mixture of colours and widths of paper. The hand-painted eggs are described on page 84.

1 Fill natural and coloured woven baskets with shredded tissue, straw and a mixture of hand-painted and chocolate eggs.

2 Fold newspaper into 1 cm/½ in-wide strips. Fix a row of strips 1 cm/½ in apart and weave other strips in and out alternately to form a flat sheet. Fold the sheet in half and glue the sides to make a bag. Tape some handles to the top. Fill with raffia, eggs and your gift.

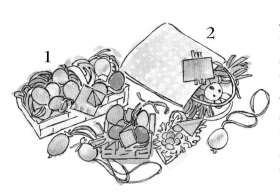

Fold a piece of paper in half to make a card. Make four narrow slits. Cut three strips of paper and decorate with egg shapes. Weave the strips in and out of the slits.

1 *Cut some pretty coloured paper into a tag shape. Cut several narrow strips in contrasting colours for the weaving.*

2 *Cut some regularly spaced slits in the tag. Weave the first strip over and under the slits. Weave the next strip under and over. Leave the ends different lengths.*

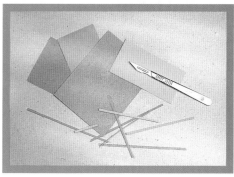

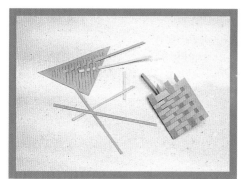

COLOURED EGGS

To blow an egg, pierce it at the top and bottom with a drawing pin and blow the contents out gently. Rinse out with water and drain on kitchen towel. Paint with coloured inks or thin paint. Use a needle to thread fine ribbon through the egg. Knot the end or tie on a bead.

RESIST EGGS

Paint a pattern on to your egg with masking fluid. When it is dry,
paint the egg, let it dry and rub off the fluid. You can also use candle
wax to resist the paint.

Chapter Eight

INDIAN IDEAS

India conjures up images of vibrant-coloured silks, intricate metal designs and the wonderful colours and smells of eastern spices. Search out specialist Indian stores that stock exquisite silks, ribbons and accessories at reasonable prices. At Christmas you will often find unusual Indian decorations such as tassels, fabric birds and metal ornaments. Give your gift wrapping an eastern look by using papers and boxes in gold and rich colours with contrasting ribbons and tags.

1 Fill a marbled carrier bag with your gifts and decorate with a silk and metal elephant charm.

2 Tie a rust and gold marbled box with metallic ribbon. Decorate with gold sequins and a metal tag.

3 Tie marbled boxes with metallic and marbled ribbons. Decorate with silk and metal ornaments.

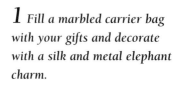

PAPERS

You can buy an amazing range of marbled papers but you can make
your own version at home. Fill a large plastic trough, about
6cm/2½in deep, with thin wallpaper paste. Mix two or three colours
of oil paint with white spirit until they are of medium consistency.
Drop spots of colour on to the paste and gently stir with a knitting
needle. Place your paper on the oil surface, lift it out and leave to dry.

TAGS

A wide selection of ornaments and tags useful for decorating your Indian-style gifts. The brightly coloured paper labels were made out of sweet wrappers - see page 91. The other ornaments were sold as Christmas decorations. Most stores now stock a wide range of unusual items imported from the East.

SWEET SURPRISE

Give an exotic look to your gift wrapping by using metallic effect boxes and papers, vibrant silk tassels, hand made sweet wrapper tags and Indian-style decorations. These unique gifts are irresistible!

1 Gather together a selection of old sweet wrappers and sequins. Draw the tag shape on to medium-weight paper (templates pages 114-127).

2 Cut out the tag. Using fast-drying, clear adhesive, stick small, torn bits of sweet papers and sequins to cover the tag.

3 Cut away the excess paper from around the tag. Punch a hole through the top and thread through fine ribbon or several strands of coloured cotton.

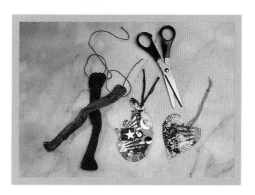

MARBLED TREASURES

Wrap a narrow strip of hand-marbled paper around a bought paper carrier bag - the marbling method is described on page 88. Decorate with coloured beads and metal charms threaded on to strands of cotton.

BIRDS OF PARADISE

Buy some boxes or paint or cover some old boxes in bright colours. Tie with metallic or bright-coloured silk ribbons. Add some tassels and bright fabric birds for extra decoration.

Chapter Nine

TASTE OF
THE ORIENT

The gifts in this section take their inspiration from the colours and textures found in the Far East. These range from natural bamboo, stones and wood to paper masks, flowers and fans in vibrant colours. Look out for unusual eastern-style boxes and containers that are used to present oriental food: a bamboo steamer filled with soaps and gifts for the bathroom makes a cheap and original gift.

1 Decorate a bamboo steamer with stones wired together and a bunch of grasses.

2 Wrap a wooden box with a leaf and a collection of coloured stones.

3 Wrap a bar of soap in recycled paper and tie with wire, stones and cane sticks.

4 Fill a wooden box with decorative glass and stones. Wrap in raffia, bamboo and grass

5 Place your gift on a sushi board and wrap with leaves, grasses, string and stones.

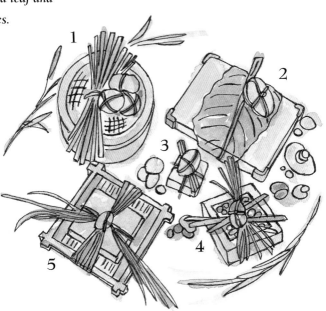

PLEATED PAPER

Pleating is a very versatile and simple technique. Sections of pleated paper make wonderful gift wrapping. Use light-weight paper that can be folded easily. Vary the widths of the pleats and the width of the paper for different effects. Keep the pleating neat and even for best results. White, textured, hand made papers look particularly effective. The delicate pleating used on the gifts opposite captures the feeling of Japanese papercraft.

1 Cut sufficient paper to wrap your box. Cut a piece of paper about twice the length of the box for pleating. Begin folding over the width of pleat you require. Make a narrow strip of pleated paper and a very small section for the matching tag.

2 Wrap the gift. Secure the large piece of pleated paper at one end. Gently twist the paper until the desired effect is achieved and stick down the other end. Add the narrower pleated strip in the same way.

COLOURFUL CREPE

Crepe papers in vibrant colours make an ordinary gift look very special.
Some crepe papers have a contrasting colour on the reverse side and
these papers come in handy for simple tags – made by folding a
rectangle of paper in half – and for tying around gifts. Pretty paper fans
make a good base for small gifts.

FESTIVE FOLDING

Cover boxes with brightly coloured crepe paper. Cut some strips of crepe
paper, in contrasting colours, long enough to go around the boxes. Hold
the paper between your thumb and finger and pull to stretch the edge of
the paper slightly. Wrap these bands around the middle of the boxes.
Decorate with Chinese paper flowers, fruit and dragons.

Chapter Ten

NOVELTY GIFT WRAPPING

The bright and jazzy look of the gifts in this section will appeal to children and adults alike. Sweets are one of the main themes – they make great gifts themselves, can be used as extra decorations and a basic sweet shape makes a fun gift tag. Try to think up fun ways of wrapping your gifts to disguise the shape of the gift itself – the pencil on page 109 is an unusual way of wrapping an odd-shaped gift. In contrast, put your gift in a clear, plastic envelope and add some flowers and paper confetti. Wrapping ordinary boxes in coloured paper and then in plain or patterned cellophane is a simple way of creating fun gift wrapping.

1 Paint or wrap a box in a bright primary colour and wrap it in cellophane. Tie with ribbon and add a papier mâché decoration.

2 Cover a box with patterned cellophane and tie with shredded ribbon and a papier mâché decoration.

3 Make the front of a box into a clock by sticking or painting on numbers. Add hands to look like a pen and pencil. Wrap in cellophane.

4 Wrap a cone-shaped gift in cellophane and tie with yellow raffia and a paper sunflower.

5 Wrap your gift in tissue paper and scrumple it into a ball. Cover with spotted cellophane and tie with raffia and a decoration.

SWEET THOUGHTS

Gifts of sweets and chocolates are always appreciated, especially if they are wrapped in an original way. Fill some cone-shaped cellophane bags with novelty sweet shapes and tie with shredded paper and net. Small gifts wrapped in coloured tissue paper in a cellophane bag look equally appealing.

STUNNING *STATIONERY*

Large envelopes or folders are cheap and make great, simple gift wrapping. Tie with contrasting string and add a novelty pen and notebook.

Fill transparent, coloured envelopes with stationery and add a few petals and bits of confetti for extra interest.

FANCY DRESS

Make a plain box a gift in itself by decorating it to look like something else! Use your imagination to create a costume appropriate to the person receiving the gift. Employ any of the paper techniques, such as pleating, curling, folding and cutting, to create truly original gift wrapping.

1 Gather together a selection of coloured papers and all the accessories you need. Wrap your box in plain white paper. Start cutting strips of grey paper 1cm/½in wide.

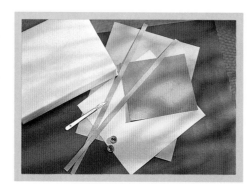

2 Wrap black paper around the box and stick down, folding back the corners for the lapels. Stick down the grey stripes and make the flower (template page 126-127) and the handkerchief.

3 Cut out two bow tie shapes (template page 126-127). Stick together with a strip of paper. Decorate the tie and fix to the box. Cut out a label and attach the buttons.

CLASHING COLOURS

Choose a paint that contrasts with the paper. Make it quite runny, dip in an old toothbrush and flick on to the paper. Decorate with paper ribbon and sweets.

Spatter a box with a clashing colour of paint and make a matching tag. Wrap with paper ribbon and add some marzipan vegetables threaded on to a wooden skewer.

BOLD AND BEAUTIFUL

Decorate some brightly coloured boxes
with contrasting braids, clusters of
sweets or Italian biscuits wrapped in
waxed papers.

Boxes in primary colours
decorated with shredded
paper and gift tags. Mix
some lollipops or
sparklers in with the
paper. Gather the paper
and decorations together
and bind at the end with
tape. Cut a small hole in
the top of the box and
push the bundle through.

PENCIL PACKAGING

A large coloured paper pencil is a novel way to
wrap a gift. Fill the pencil with novelty bits of
stationery and sweets or perhaps a T-shirt, scarf
or gloves. Fill the end of the pencil with crumpled
tissue paper. Make a contrasting pencil gift tag.

*1 Cut out a yellow rectangle 25
x 28cm/10 x 11in in medium-
weight paper. Cut out the point of
the pencil from white and yellow
paper (see templates page
126-127).*

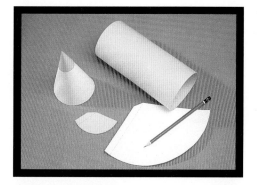

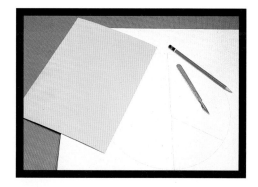

*2 Make the rectangle into a tube
and glue down the edge. Make the
yellow and white points into two
cones, making sure they fit inside the
end of the tube. Stick the yellow cone
over the white cone.*

*3 Make a contrasting pencil tag
and thread through some plastic
thread. Push the top of the pencil
into the tube and secure inside
with sticky tape.*

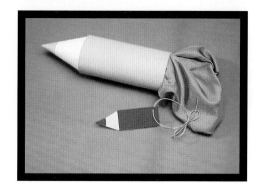

Gift Wrappings
TEMPLATES

TEMPLATES

TEMPLATES

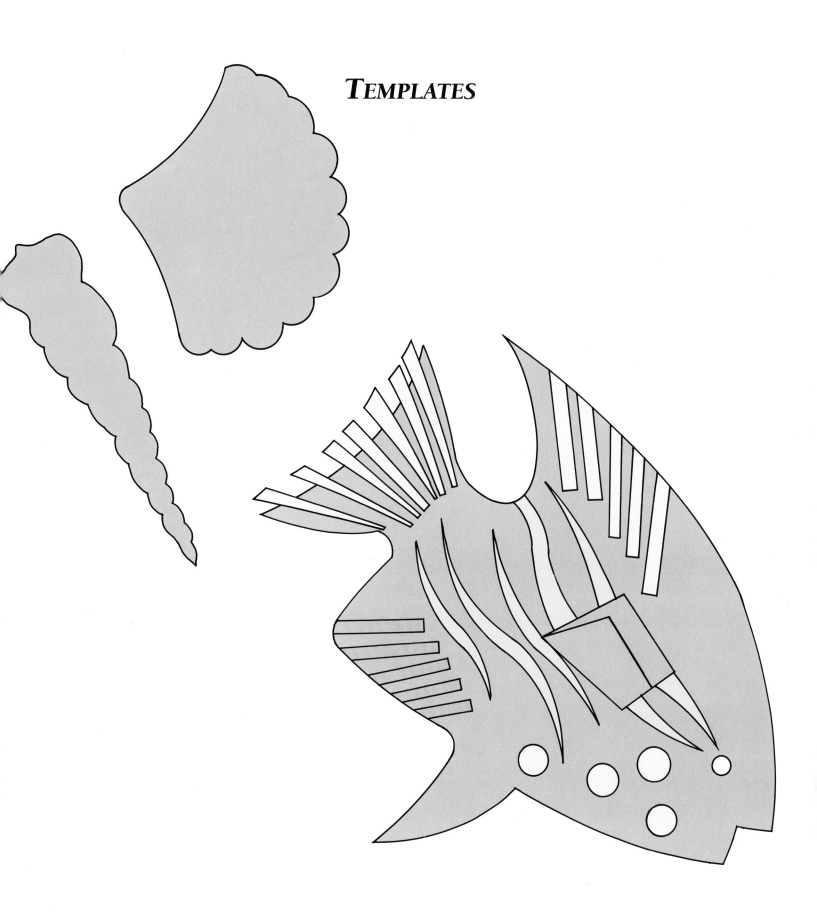

TEMPLATES

TEMPLATES

TEMPLATES

TEMPLATES

TEMPLATES

TEMPLATES

TEMPLATES

HALF SIZE

TEMPLATES

TEMPLATES

TEMPLATES

TEMPLATES

HALF SIZE

TEMPLATES